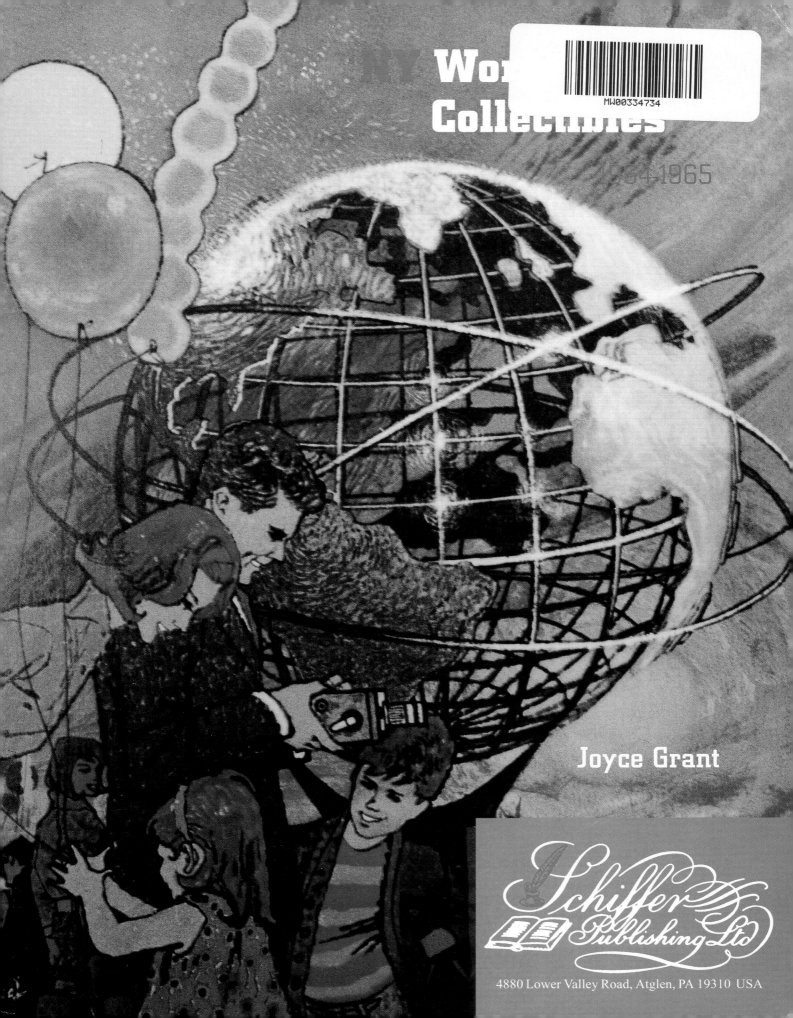

Wo...
Collectibles

...64-1965

Joyce Grant

Schiffer Publishing Ltd

4880 Lower Valley Road, Atglen, PA 19310 USA

Dedication

This book is dedicated to Mom & Dad, who took me to the Fair.

Designed by Bonnie M. Hensley
Type set in Americana XBd BT/Souvenir Lt BT

ISBN: 0-7643-0732-0
Printed in China
1 2 3 4 T

Published by Schiffer Publishing Ltd.
4880 Lower Valley Road
Atglen, PA 19310
Phone: (610) 593-1777; Fax: (610) 593-2002
E-mail: Schifferbk@aol.com
Please visit our web site catalog at www.schifferbooks.com

In Europe, Schiffer books are distributed by
Bushwood Books
6 Marksbury Rd. Kew Gardens
Surrey TW9 4JF England
Phone: 44 (0)181 392-8585; Fax: 44 (0)181 392-9876
E-mail: Bushwd@aol.com

This book may be purchased from the publisher.
Please include $3.95 for shipping. Please try your bookstore first. We are interested
in hearing from authors with book ideas on related subjects.
You may write for a free catalog.

Contents

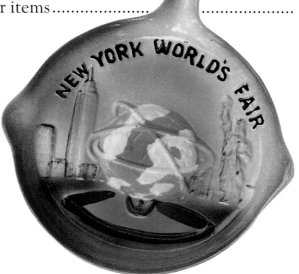

Acknowledgments

First of all, I would like to acknowledge Peter Schiffer & his staff for their support & the opportunity to do this book. The following people have proved invaluable to me in this endeavor– for finding me World's Fair items or for allowing me to photograph their collections: David Audet, Erik Jensen, Bruce Tannin, Pat & Charlie Cangelosi, Mike Pender, Betty Abromowitz, Al Ackerman, Bill Blair, John Schoonmaker & especially Norman Hulme. Thanks also to my pal & business partner Karen Binder for her help & for putting up with my "Fair mania," and also, to Abby Ruoff for her support & advice. A special thanks to my children, Andrea & Jared, for their tolerance & help. A very special thanks to my wonderful husband, Brian, whose support & encouragement throughout this project has made it so much easier.

Introduction

One of the best things about growing up in the sixties was a trip to the NY World's Fair. I was 8 - 9 years old then, but I remember clearly "typing" on the IBM Selectric typewriter (such an amazing machine at the time), molding my own dinosaur at the Sinclair Attraction (I can still smell the plastic melting), and being able to talk on a telephone while actually seeing the person I was talking to (just like the Jetsons!).

The purpose of this book is to help us relive those days at the fair by showing the huge array of souvenirs available to the visitors. The toys were the best! For the kids, there were flashlights, dinosaurs, hats, and spinning toys to name a few. There were aprons and household items for Mom, and pen sets and cufflinks for Dad.

There were thousands of souvenirs marketed at the Fair. Every pavilion had its own, plus the many paper products, china, and toys that were available at the souvenir stands. Not to mention the free brochures and pins that were given out at all the attractions. This book will show a portion of them. You will also see items used in the everyday operations of the Fair; some are one-of-a-kind items highly sought after by collectors.

An approximate value is listed with each item, reflecting the Fair market value, which is based on the actual price paid for the item. Prices account for items in mint or near mint condition. Souvenirs in their original package will, naturally, bring a much higher price. A "+" after the amount indicates the item is rare or very desirable and the value could be more. Prices have been compiled from a combination of sources: retail prices from dealers, World's Fair collectibles shows, and correspondence with collectors. With internet access today, sellers are able to reach a wider audience and in turn may achieve higher prices on their rare World's Fair collectibles. On the other side of the spectrum, common items are getting a much lower price on the internet, because they are easier to find. Many items shown in this book can still be purchased at a fraction of the market value. Flea Markets and yard sales provide a mecca for great finds at budget prices.

So, come relive those days at the fair when we were on the brink of the computer and technology age—before touch tone, ATM's, CD's, answering machines, and email, when Cousin Brucie was still spinning the Beatles tunes. It was 1964 and time to go to the Fair, the one place you didn't mind going with your parents.

The idea for the 1964-65 NY World's Fair was first conceived in 1958 by Robert Koppel, a New York Lawyer. He felt that children needed to learn something about the world. In 1960, Robert Moses replaced Koppel as the President of the Fair Corporation.

Robert Moses, a City Planner & the NYC Parks Commissioner, received support from the city and state to build the Fair in Flushing Meadows Park, Queens (the site of the 1939-40 World's Fair). His hope was to use the Fair's profits to build a Museum of Science, a Zoo, and a Botanical Garden.

The Fair had 175 pavilions which were built on 643 acres. Robert Moses wanted the Fair to include "something for everyone." The theme for the Fair was "Peace Through Understanding," dedicated to "Mans Achievements On A Shrinking Globe In An Expanding Universe." 51 million people visited the Fair during its two-year run from May 22 to October 10, 1964, and May 21 to October 17, 1965.

The Fair was divided into 5 major areas: Industrial, International, Federal & State, and Transportation & Lake/Amusement Areas. Souvenirs from these areas are usually marked with the name of the pavilion on them. Items purchased at kiosks, or souvenir stands, on the midway or in souvenir shops have the *Unisphere* logo and were licensed by the Fair. Another logo added to many of the toys available was Peter & Wendy - the Fair twins.

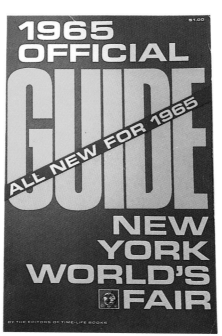

Official Guide books. Soft cover, 5" x 8". 1964 edition: $22-25. 1965: $18-22.

Official Guide book. Hardcover edition, $100+.

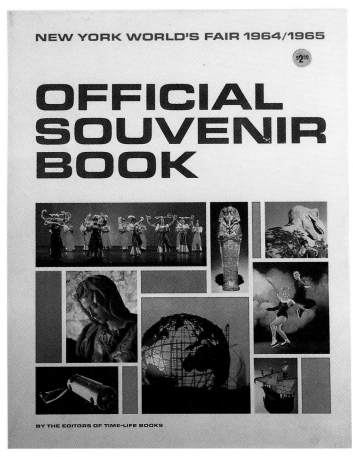

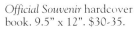
Official Souvenir hardcover
book. 9.5" x 12". $30-35.

Official 3" x 3.5" flag
on card. $55-60.

Felt Pennant. 18". $20-25.

Official red carpet. 5" long. $40-45.

Pinback. 3" diameter. $25-30.

Souvenir medal in 2.5" x 3.5" box. $28-30.

Miss New York doll. 13" tall. $175-200.

Child's Flicker badge. Plastic, 3" diameter. $28-35.

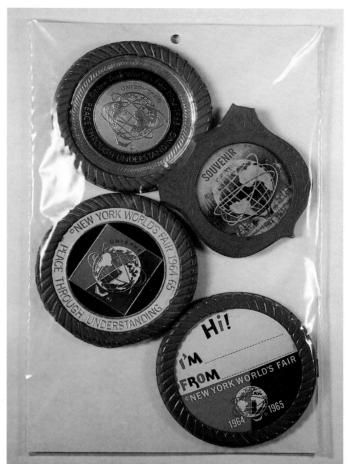

Assorted plastic flicker pins. 2.5" diameter. $18-25 ea.

Assorted metal pins. 0.5" - 1.5" diameter. $12-15 ea.

Metal pinback. 3.5" diameter. $35-40.

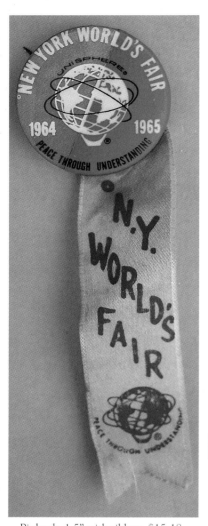

Pinback. 1.5" with ribbon. $15-18.

Souvenir book. Hardcover, 8.5" x 11". $20-25.

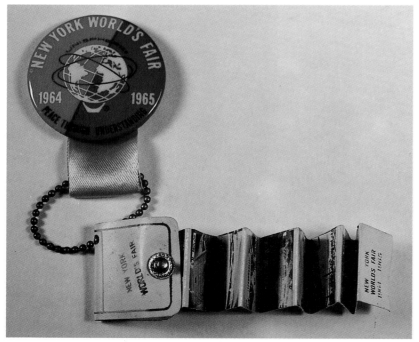

Pinback. 1.5" diameter with foldout photos. $20-25.

Souvenir booklet. Soft cover, 8.5" x 11". $12-15.

NYS Vacationguide. Soft cover, 8" x 11". $10-12.

Sheet music. $25-30.

Christmas gift envelope for admission tickets. $18-20.

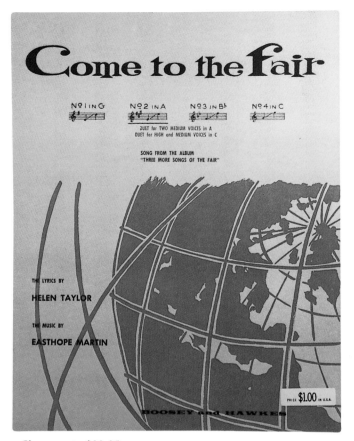

Sheet music. $40-50.

Sheet music. $30-35.

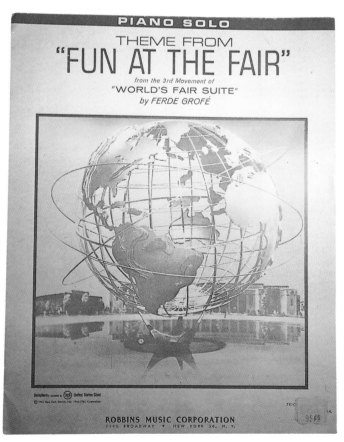

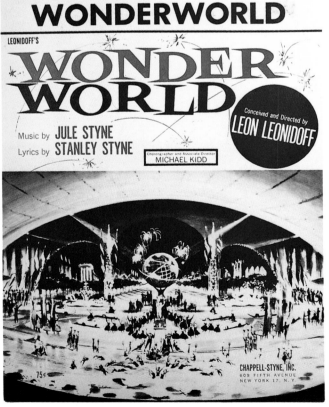

Sheet music. $30-35.

Sheet music. $25-30.

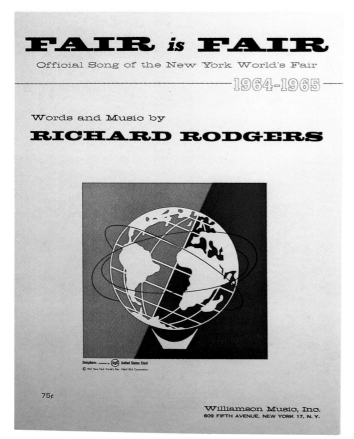

Sheet music. $35-40.

Record. 45rpm. $35-45.

Metal buildings paperweight. 5" long. $40-55+.

Postcard booklet. $10-12.

Mini photo book. 3" x 5". $10-12.

Mini postcard book. 2.5" x 3.5". $5-8.

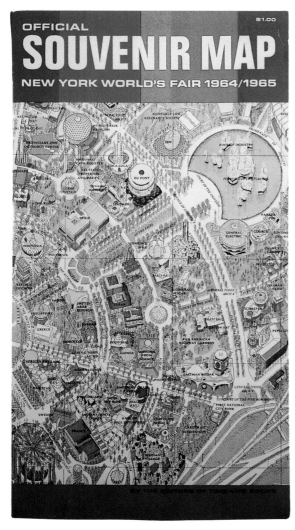

Souvenir map, front view. $20-28.

Souvenir map, open view.

Fold out postcards. $10-15 ea.

Postcard. 3" x 5". $3-5.

Assorted postcards. $3-5 ea.

Assorted greeting cards.
4" x 10". $8-10 ea.

Assorted decals & stickers. $25-30 ea.

Silk bookmark. 5" long. $18-20.

Viewmaster reels with envelopes. $18-25 ea.

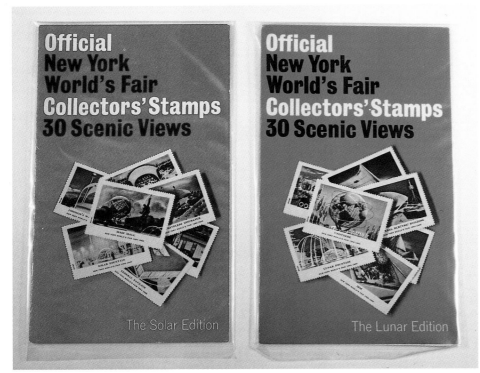

Collector stamp sets. 8" x 5". $18-20 ea.

Assorted decals. $18-22 ea.

Mini flashcards. 3.5" x 2.5". $18-22.

Metal wastebasket. 11" tall. $85-95+.

Large paper shopping bag. $18-20.

Bumper sticker. 5" x 16". $15-22.

Elephant bank. Plastic, 11" tall. $75-125+.

Chalkware bank. 9" tall. $225-300+.

Metal bank. 5" tall. $40-45.

Ceramic bank. 6" tall. $65-75.

Metal bank. Penny on top. 4.5" tall. $45-50.

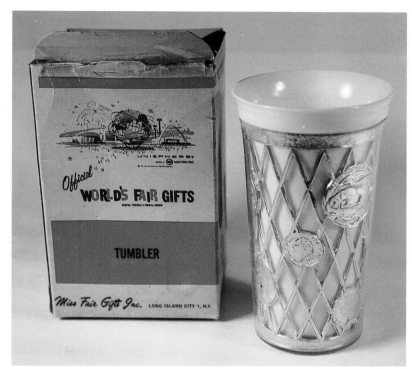

Plastic 6" tall tumbler with box. $45-50.

Daily Dime registering bank. Metal, 3" x 3". $65-75+.

Plastic 6" tall bank with box. $45-55.

Frosted glass with wood handle. 5.5" tall. $10-12.

Plastic dish. 4" diameter. $10-12.

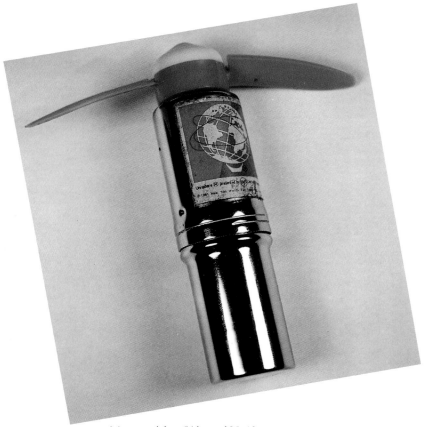

Motorized fan. 5" long. $28-40.

Mini cup & saucer. 1" x 2". $45-50.

TV picture viewer. 2.5" x 1.5". $18-28.

Unisphere Picture Viewer on 5.5" x 3.5" card. $55-60.

Slides & folding viewer in mailing
envelope. $30-35.

Slides & viewer in plastic box. $35-40.

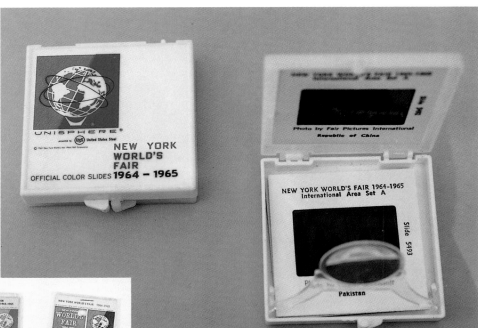

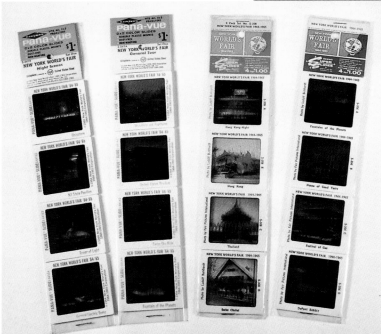

Slides in original package. 2" x 10". $15-18 ea.

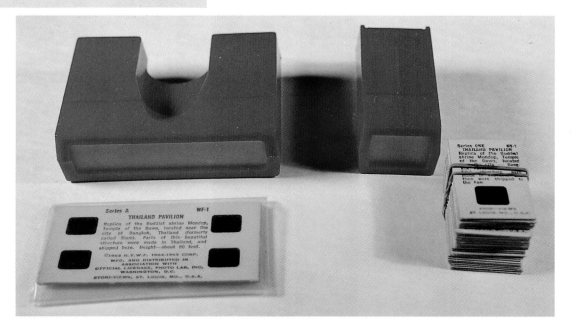

Viewers & slide sets. $35-40 ea.

Kodak camera with box. $85-90.

School bookcovers in original package. 9.75" x 13". $35-40.

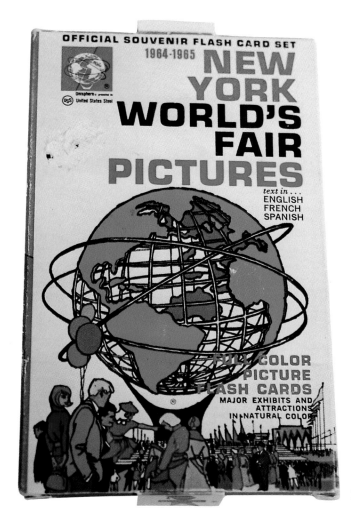

Flash cards in box. 4" x 6". $15-18.

Playing cards in box. $35-40.

Weather card. 3" x 5". $5-10.

Bridge card set in box. $20-28.

Jim Beam liquor decanter. $65-85.

Set of wood coasters. $12-15.

Assorted metal & glass coasters. $30-35 per set.

Set of wood coasters with holder. $35-40.

Hotplate set - treated cardboard. $18-22.

Large tablecloth. $125-150+.

Cocktail set - outside view. $175-200.

Egg timer. Metal, 3" tall. $75-85+.

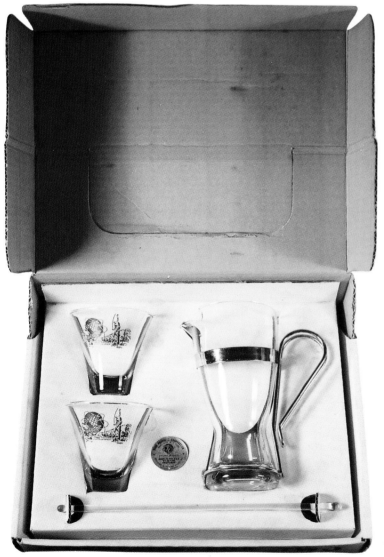

Cocktail set, inside view.

Metal mirror. 6" long. $18-25.

Metal 3" bell with box. $45-50.

Flower arranger. Metal, 14" tall. $150-175+.

Plant sticks, closed view. 7" x 10". $65-75+.

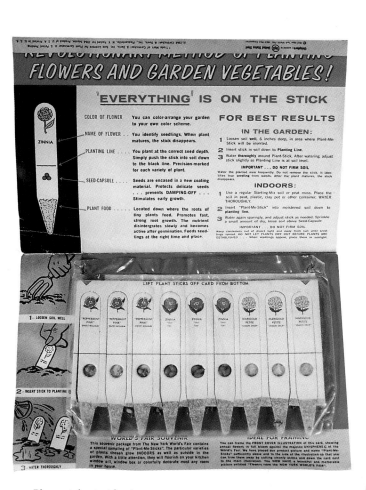

Plant sticks, inside view.

Toothpick holder with box. Metal, 3" tall. $35-45.

Lady pin cushion. 9.5" tall. $30-40+.

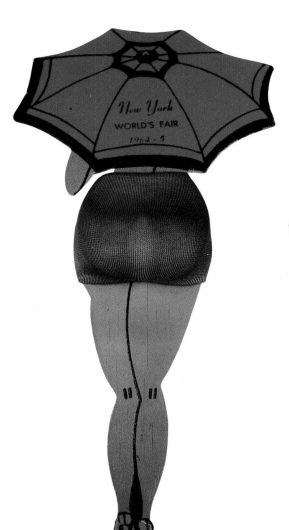

Tin recipe box. 3.5" x 5". $30-40.

Cloth hostess apron with
original bag. $55-65.

Placemat set in original
bag. 17.5" x 11.5". $45-65.

Plastic salad server set in 11" box. $40-45.

Cedar jewelry boxes. $30-40 ea.

Cedar jewelry box. 5.5" x 3.5". $30-40.

Plastic cocktail forks in original 3.5" box. $30-35.

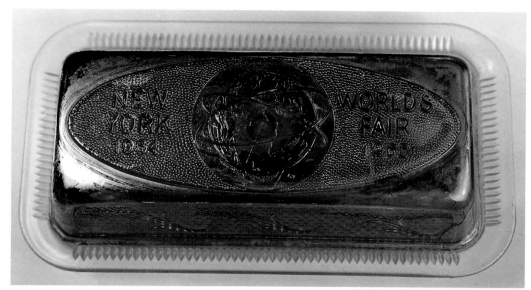

Plastic butter dish with cover. $10-18.

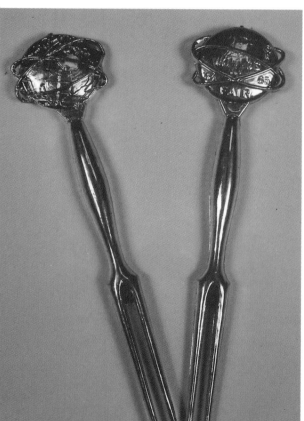

Dial soaps. 1.5" x 2.5". $25-30 ea.

Plastic cocktail forks. 3" long. $2-3 ea.

Tea bag. $35-40.

Domino sugar package. 2.5" x 1.5". $28-35.

Sugar cube. 1.25" x 0.75". $28-40.

Metal salt & pepper shaker with tray in original box. $35-40.

Paper napkin & coaster set in box. $18-25.

Salt & pepper with box. $30-35.

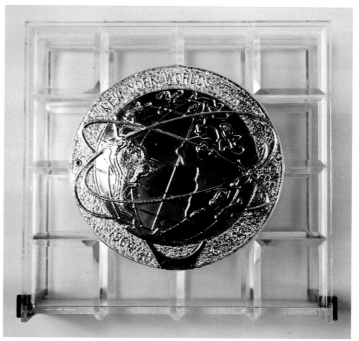

Plastic napkin holder. 5" x 5". $15-20.

Wood salt & pepper. $18-22.

Paper napkins in original wrapper. 10" x 10". $20-25.

Metal memo pad. 5" x 3". $20-22.

Desk set with Parker pen. $125-150+.

Lucite paperweight. 6" long. $30-35.

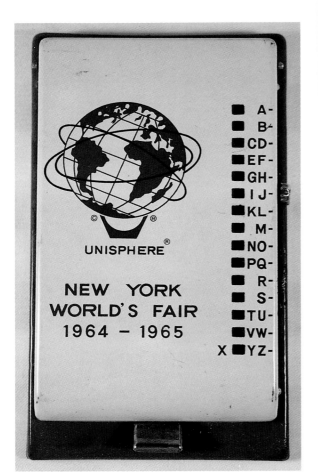

Metal phone directory. 6.5" x 3". $40-45.

Pencil set in box. 8" long. $30-35.

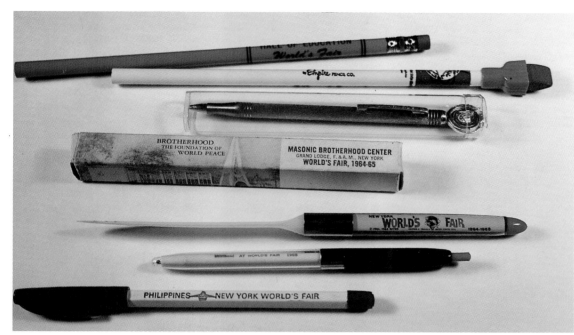

Assorted pens & pencils.
$10-20 ea.

Lucite paperweights with early
Unisphere design. $35-45 ea.

Unisphere metal pencil sharp-
ener. 2" tall. $18-22.

Stationery in original box. 6" x 8". $45-50.

Insurance company portfolio. Vinyl, 4.5" x 10". $25-30.

Stationery in original box. 6" x 8". $45-50.

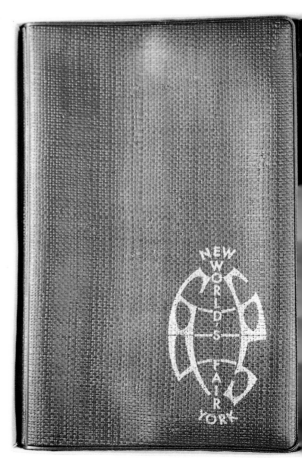

Vinyl bookcover. 5" x 8". $35-40.

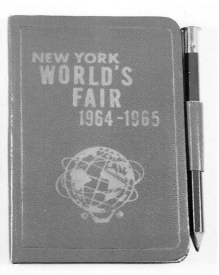

Two memo pads, one with pencil. 4" x 2.5". $20-25 ea.

Vinyl memo pad. 4.5" x 3". $12-18.

Mini photo album. 3" x 4". $12-18.

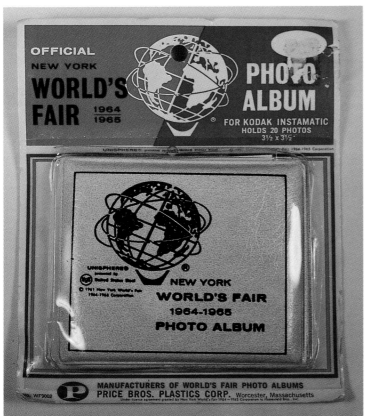

Mini photo album on 7.5" x 6" card. $40-50.

Mallory key light in box. $50-55.

NY subway token holder keychain. $45-50.

Hasbro vinyl autograph book. 5" x 6". $65-75.

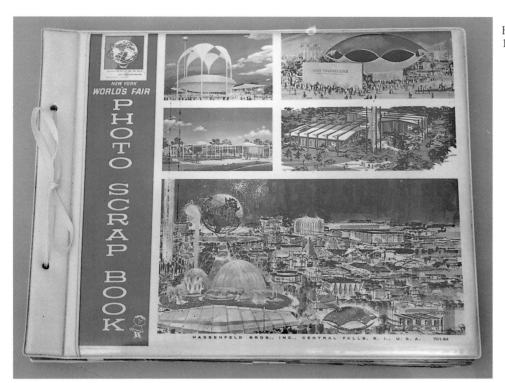

Hasbro vinyl scrapbook.
11" x 14". $75-95.

Mallory key chain
light. $25-30.

Electric plug-in night light. Plastic,
2.5" x 3". $100-150+.

Mallory key case light. 3" x 2". $25-30.

Unisphere keychain on
card. $20-25.

Jack knife on 3" x 5" card. $55-65.

Jack knife on 3" x 5" card
with chain. $65-75.

Key on keychain. $15-18.

Key on keychain with cards. $25-30 ea.

His & Hers keychains in box. $45-55.

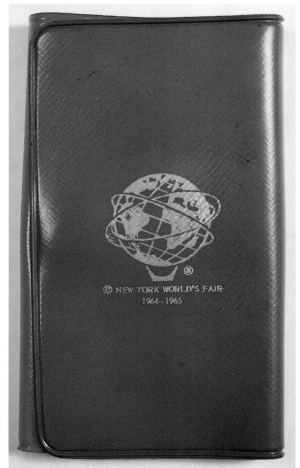

Key purse. 4" x 2". $8-10.

Assorted keychains. $15-45 ea.

Adult vinyl rain cape. $85-95.

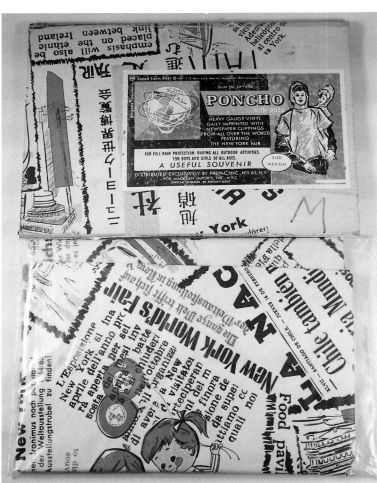

Vinyl poncho in cardboard box. $50-55.

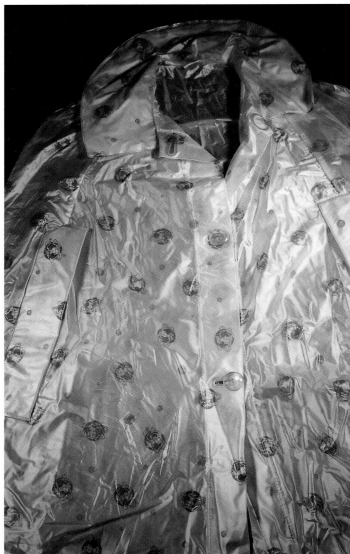

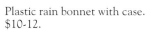
Plastic rain bonnet with case.
$10-12.

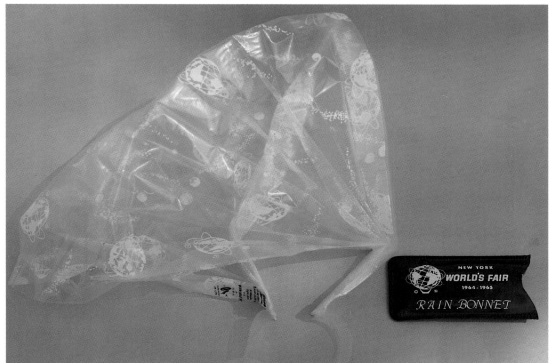

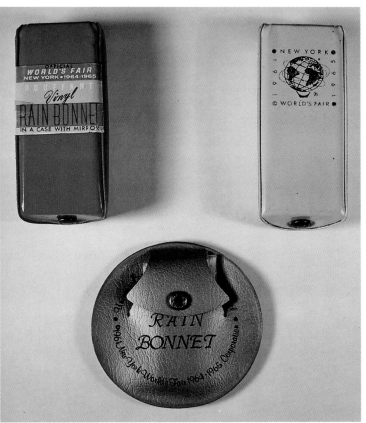

Assorted rain bonnets in cases. $15-18 ea.

Child's hat. $25-38.

Felt Swiss hat. Child's size. $75-85.

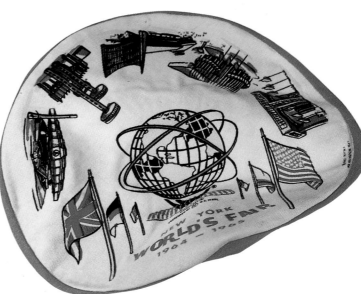

Scottish tam or beret. 9" diameter. $60-65.

Child's size hats. $25-30 ea.

Bowtie. 3.5" wide. $25-30.

String ties. $25-30 ea.

Child's sweatshirt in
original bag. $45-55.

Child's sleeveless shirt.
20" x 21". $50-55.

Vinyl tote bag. 16" x 10". $65-75.

Vinyl belt with metal medallions. $55-65.

Assorted vinyl belts. $75-95.

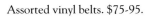

Plastic string purse, closed. $15-25.

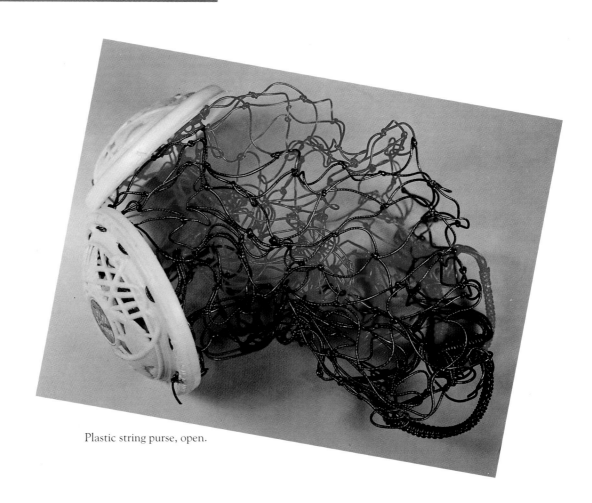

Plastic string purse, open.

Six frosted glasses with
original box. 6" tall. $80-95.

Plate, back view
showing close-up
of sticker.

Ceramic plate. 8" diameter. $10-12.

Plate, front view. 10"
diameter. $12-15.

Ceramic snack set. $50-55.

Candy dish in original box. 7" diameter. $45-50.

Beer stein. 6" tall. $30-40.

Coffee Hound cup. 4" x 4.5". $20-40.

Ceramic plate. 10" diameter. $10-12.

Silverplated 4" spoon with original box. $20-22.

Ceramic 6" spoon rest. $20-25.

Assorted demitasse spoons. $20-25 ea.

Plastic plaque with original box. 7" diameter. $45-50.

Wood serving tray. 10.5" diameter. $20-22.

Tin tray. 8" diameter. $5-10.

Foil art picture. 8" x 10". $15-18.

Tin Litho Tip tray. 4" x 6". $6-8.

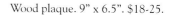
Wood plaque. 9" x 6.5". $18-25.

Ceramic bookends. 5" tall. $65-75.

Matchbook. $3-4.

Long matchbook. $10-15.

Pair of matchbooks. $5-6.

Unisphere matchbooks with box. $45-50.

Mini Japan lighter. 1" x 1.5". $55-60.

Japan flip top lighter. $55-60.

Scripto Vu-lighter. $150-185+.

Lighter. 2" x 1.5". $80-95.

Table lighter. 3" x 2". $150-175+.

Ceramic ashtray. 7" x 5". $10-12.

Ceramic ashtray with metal rings. 5" tall. $35-40.

Metal ashtray. 5.5" tall. $25-30.

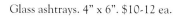
Glass ashtrays. 4" x 6". $10-12 ea.

Tin ashtray. 3.5" x 3.5". $2-5.

Mini glass ashtrays in original box. 2.25" x 2.25" ea. $28-35 set.

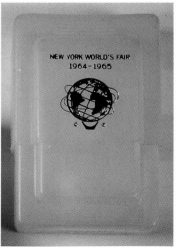

Plastic cigarette cases.
$10-12 ea.

Molded plastic *Unisphere*. 3.5" tall. $65-75.

Metal flip calendar. 3" tall. $35-50.

Plastic *Unisphere*. 3" tall. $20-25.

Bobbing *Unisphere* with box. 5" tall. $60-65.

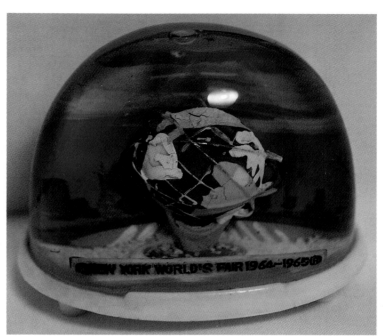

Snowdome. 3.5" tall. $35-40.

Snowdome. 4.5" tall. $35-45.

Collapsible plastic cups. $18-20 ea.

Frosted glass candle. 9" tall. $35-45.

Sticker. 9" x 9". $35-40.

Towel. 17" x 26". $55-65.

Silk Scarf. 24" x 24". $55-60.

Handkerchiefs. 13" x 13". $30-35 ea.

Towel set, outside view. $65-76.

Towel set, inside view.

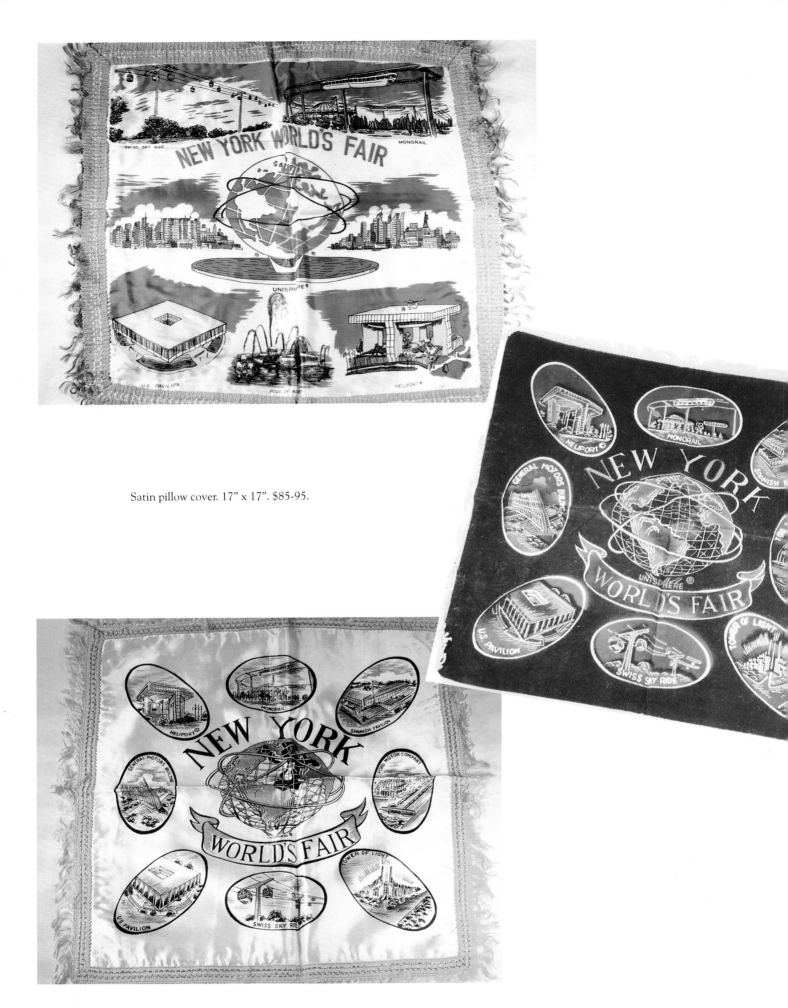

Satin pillow cover. 17" x 17". $85-95.

Car medallion. Plastic stick-on, 3.25" diameter. $15-18.

Bicycle license plate. Metal, 3" x 5". $25-30.

Car license plate. Metal, 11" x 6". $85-95.

Bicycle license plates. Metal, 3" x 5". $25-30.

Laminated license plate. 11" x 6". $35-45.

Car medallion. Metal, 3" diameter. $45-50.

Pill or snuff box. 1.5" x 3.75". $30-35.

Heart shape metal dish in original box. 5" wide. $28-30.

Pill box with flicker picture. Metal, 1.5" x 1.5". $25-35.

Metal ashtray in original box.
3.5". $20-25.

Mirrored paperweight. 3" x 3". $15-20.

Metal dish. 4.25" diameter. $10-12.

Metal covered box. 2.5" x 1.5".
$28-30.

Mini purse with keychain. 2.5" x 2". $15-20.

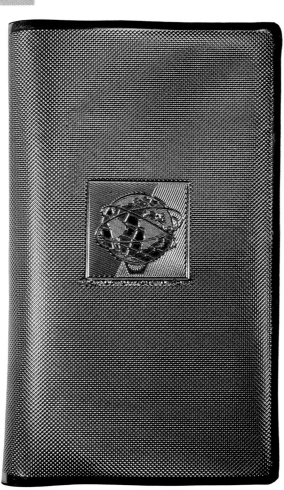

Grooming kit & wallet,
outside view. $18-20.

Grooming kit & wallet, inside view.

Vinyl makeup case. 6" wide. $18-25.

Rubber squeeze purses. 3" long. $15-20 ea.

His & Hers key cases. 2.5" x 3.5". $15-20 ea.

Photo wallet. 4" x 3". $18-20.

Coin purse with keychain. 3" x 2". $25-30.

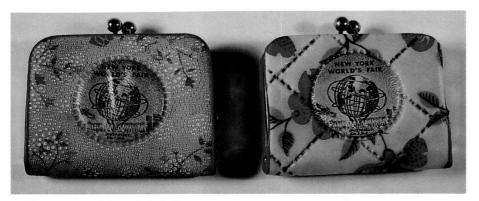

Change purses. 2.5" x 2". $18-25 ea.

Billfold. 3.5" x 3". $30-35.

Leather change purse. 4.5" wide. $45-55.

Assorted vinyl wallets. 4" x 3". $15-18 ea.

Vinyl billfold. 4" x 3". $5-10.

Compact with lipstick holder. $85-95+.

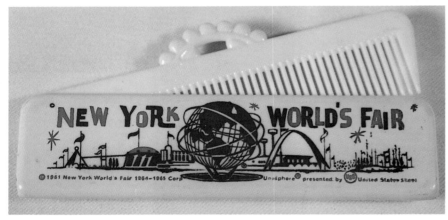

Mirror & comb kit. 4" wide. $25-30.

Heart shaped compact with box. 3" wide. $95-105+.

Pocket mirror. 2.5" x 3.5". $12-18.

Cufflinks. $8-12.

Money clip on 2.5" x 3" card. $40-45.

Pendant watches (one with original chain). 1.5" diameter. $250-350+ ea.

Sterling silver tie clip & cufflink
set with original box. $85-95.

Wrist watch.
$275-300+.

Money clip. $10-12.

Souvenir pin on 2.5" x 2.5" card. $35-45.

Metal belt buckles. $35-40 ea.

Sweater guards. $30-45.

Assorted pendants. $25-35 ea.

Nail clipper, locket & money clips. $25-35 ea.

Assortment of men's jewelry. $25-35 per set.

Assortment of charms.
$25-35 ea.

Assortment of
pins. $65-75 ea.

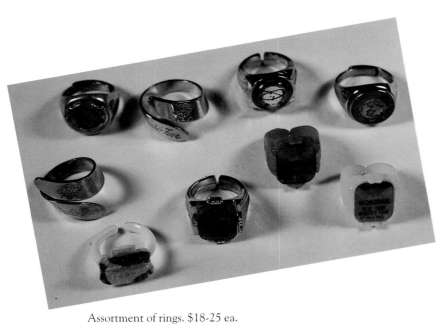

Assortment of rings. $18-25 ea.

Bracelets on cards. $65-85 ea.

Assortment of bracelets. $35-50 ea.

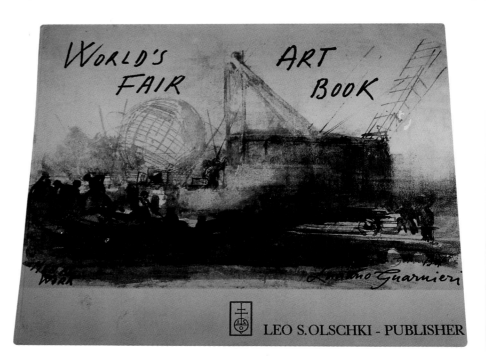

Art book, construction of World's Fair. $40-50+.

Locket on 3.5" x 7.5" card. $85-95.

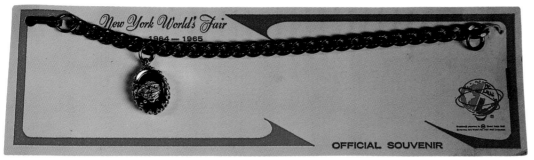

Bracelet on card. $55-65.

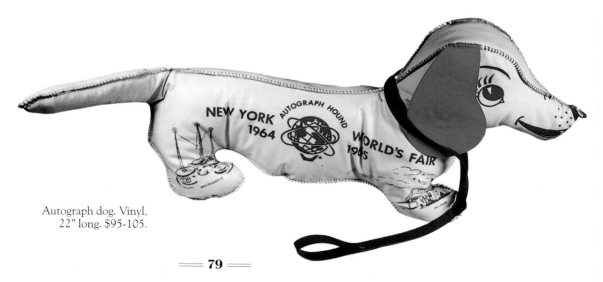

Autograph dog. Vinyl,
22" long. $95-105.

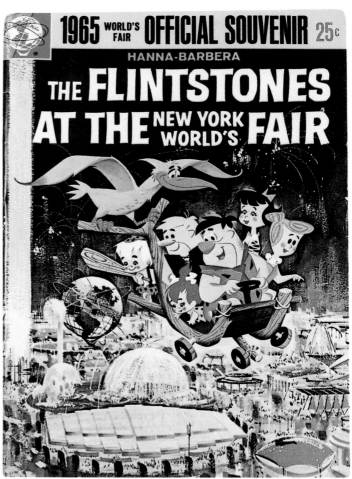

Make-A-Model book. 10" x 14". $35-40.

Flintstones comic book. $20-28.

Milton Bradley
boardgame. $75-95.

Foster Grant sunglasses on card. $65-75.

Slide puzzle on 6" x 5" card. $65-75.

Tin binoculars with compass. 4" x 4". $35-48.

Wood pop gun. 12" long. $28-30.

Children's pop-up book. 10" x 14". $40-45.

Children's pop-up book, inside view.

Everything in the Federal and State areas had delighted Peter and Wendy. And that included a delicious lunch at the New York State Pavilion. They'd had a wonderful view of the Fair from an observation tower 200 feet high.

Inside the New York City Pavilion, the Dick Button Ice Show had proved a great success. And, wonder of wonders! they'd seen Lindbergh's "Spirit of St. Louis" in the Missouri Pavilion. How tiny that plane had seemed, to carry a brave young pilot alone across the ocean!

"The breathtaking Federal Pavilion was best of all," Peter claimed, "anyway, it was the biggest!" "And all made of little pieces of colored glass!" said Wendy. "My, it shined so!" But Mother wanted to go and see the Unisphere. "After all," she said, "the Unisphere is the symbol of the Fair, so we should have a really good look at it, don't you think?"

Children's pop-up book, inside view.

Children's hardcover book. 8.5" x 11". $18-25.

It was a day of wonders! Peter and Wendy had started the wonderful day by coming from New York City to the Fair grounds by helicopter, the most exciting trip they'd ever had. And now they were actually here – it was the day they'd dreamed about for a whole year.

Already, they had visited General Motors and had taken a magic car ride outside and inside the Ford Motor Company Pavilion. "We saw past, present and future," said Peter. "How would you have liked to live in prehistoric times?" Father asked, as they came to the Sinclair Oil Company's exhibit. "This is Dinoland." Peter looked up at the 70 foot Tyrannosaurus and all he could say was "Golly." When the huge creature moved its great head and body, it was easy to imagine that it was alive. Father assured the twins that it wasn't alive, though, and Wendy plucked up enough courage to go close enough to touch. Peter finally found his voice, and announced that he'd have liked to live in the times when Dinosaurs and other great beasts might be met around any corner. "I'd slice off their heads with a sword," he said, "and carry them home to Wendy." "No thanks," said Wendy, politely.

Children's pop-up book, inside view.

Puzzle set. $35-40.

Telescope with compass. 20" long. $65-75.

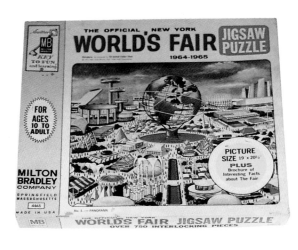

Jigsaw Puzzles. $28-32 ea.

Plastic binoculars. 5" tall. $25-30.

Party card game. 13" x 11". $85-96.

Peter & Wendy kissing nodders. 5" tall. $85-95+ pair.

Viewer & slides on original 5" x 7.5" card. $48-55.

Peter & Wendy bells. 5" tall.
$40-48 pair.

Viewer slides on 5"x 7.5" card. $40-45.

Educards card game. 4" x 5" box. $15-18.

Vinyl zippered purse. 5" x 5". $25-28.

Peter & Wendy salt & pepper
shakers. $55-75+.

Paper & wood parasol. 30" diameter. 85-95+.

Hasbro cardboard pencil box. 8.5" x 4". $30-38.

Pencil set on original card, $28-38.
One sheet of writing paper, $2-3.

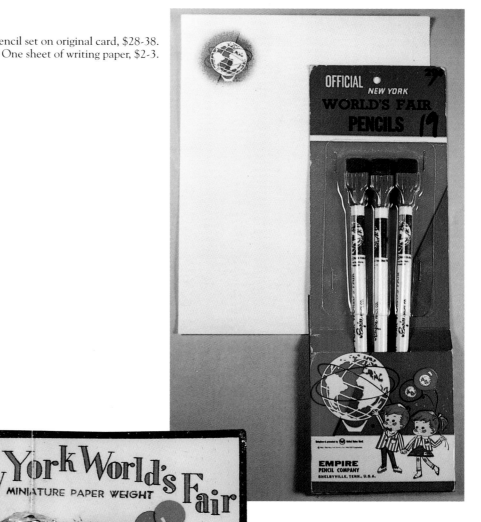

Pencil & eraser set on 9.5" x 3" card. $55-60.

Mini metal paperweight on 2" x 3" card. $45-50.

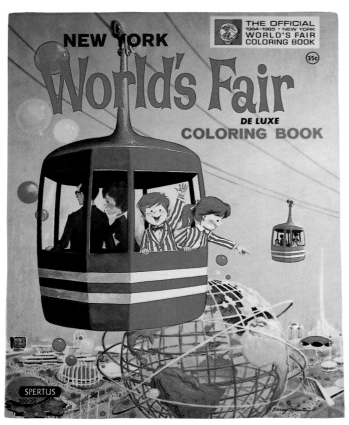

Coloring book. 8.5" x 11. $15-25.

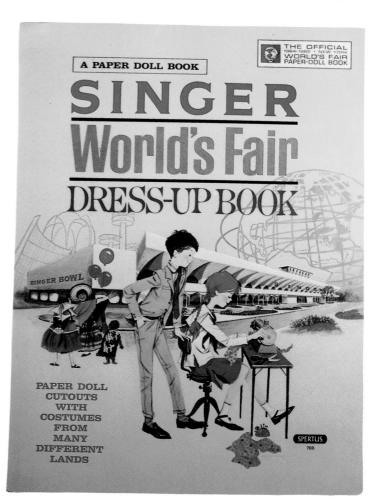

Singer paper doll book. 10" x 14". $65-70.

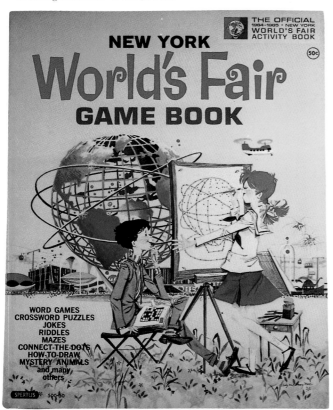

Activity/Game book. 8.5" x 11". $18-22.

Inflatable beach ball in original bag. $55-65.

Spinning toy on 7"x 12" card. $65-85.

Ice cream soda glass. 5" tall. $18-20.

Lollypop box. 8" x 5". $50-55+.

Plastic child's belt. $75-85.

Flip top flashlight. 3" long. $45-55.

Jumbo coloring book. 11" x 14". $18-25.

Lariat flashlight on 8.5" x 4" card. $75-85.

Mallory wand flashlight. 18" long. $85-95.

Child's vinyl wallet.
4.5" x 4". $65-70.

Hardcover WF book.
7" x 8". $20-25.

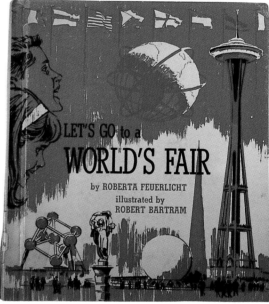

Paint set. 15" x 11.5". $125-135.

Triangular vinyl purse. 3" x
3" x 3". $10-20.

Child's vinyl wallet. 4.5" x 3". $45-65.

OFFICIAL 1964 – 1965 NEW YORK WORLD'S FAIR CHILDREN'S BOOKS

Metal book sign. 12" x 5". $65-75.

Official record album.
Davison Record Co.
$25-30.

Lofts candy mold. 13.5" x 6". $300-325+.

School luggage tag. $12-15.

Good Housekeeping Cookbook. Hardcover, 6" x 9.5". $30-40.

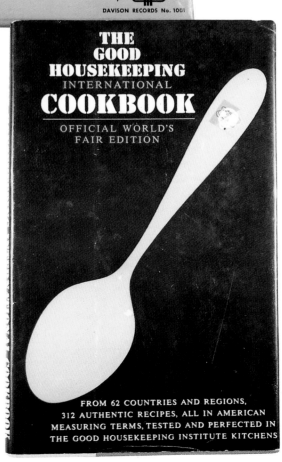

Johnny Carson record album. Columbia Records. $30-35.

Silhouette frame. 5" x 7". $18-20.

Woman's blouse. $95-125+.

Woman's blouse. $100-125+.

T-shirts. $75-95 ea.

Vinyl bag. 5" x 5". $65-75.

Woman's blouse. $125-150+.

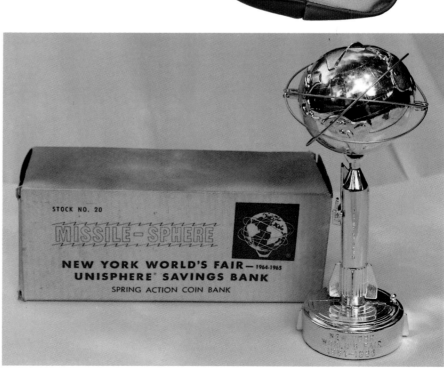

Mechanical Bank with box. Metal, 11"
tall. $500-600+.

Mini ceramic bowl & pitcher. 5" tall. $25-45.

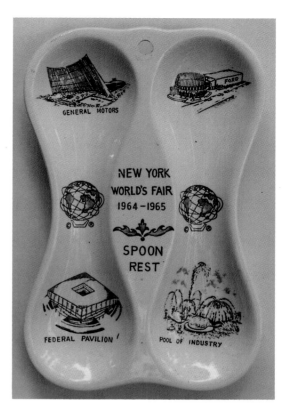

Ceramic spoon rest. 8.5" long. $28-30.

Ceramic spoon rests or wall plaques. 7" tall. $35-55 ea.

Souvenir plate with paper label. 3.25" diameter. $18-25.

Pot holder. 5" x 5". $35-45.

Metal pin dishes. 3.5" x 3.75". $35-40 ea.

Stuffed tiger. 8" x 11". $125-150+.

Baby bib. $95-100.

Lighter. $85-95.

Rubber WF Twin dolls. 8" tall. $65-85 ea.

The Industrial Area represented a showcase for American technology and products. Everywhere you turned, there was a modern wonder to see – from Bell Telephone Picturephones, to new animated life-like figures. The most popular attractions for visitors to the Industrial Area were:

IBM

A moving 500-seat "People Wall" lifts visitors into an egg-shaped theater for a multiscreen 12-minute movie, showing how computers and the human mind solve problems in much the same way.

Pepsi Cola

"It's A Small World" by Walt Disney. Visitors ride in boats through animated miniature settings of many lands.

Parker Pen

Visitors have a computer choose pen pals for them.

Travelers Insurance

Visitors walk past dioramas that dramatize the story of life on Earth.

Tower of Light

World's most powerful searchlight. Musical show featuring Reddy Kilowatt who introduces Ben Franklin to the modern uses of electricity.

General Cigar Hall of Magic

Huge smoke rings are emitted from the building, and inside there are 12-minute magic shows every half hour.

General Electric Carousel of Progress

Seated visitors are carried past a 4-part circular stage on which animated human figures act out the story of electricity from the 1890s to the 1960s and beyond. Developed by Walt Disney.

Clairol

Women could look in a mirrored device to see themselves with different hair colors.

Bell System

Visitors seated in moving armchairs with built-in stereo speakers see films and three-dimensional scenes of the history of communication.

Better Living Center

Displays of fashion, furnishings, and food. Visitors may also meet Elsie the Cow.

Eastman Kodak

On top of the pavilion are huge color prints and a moondeck for picture-taking. Inside are film and movie exhibits.

American Express

Million Dollar Money Tree on display outside the pavilion.

Avis

Visitors drive miniature autos along a scenic road.

Other Industrial Area Pavilions Included:

Arlington Hat, Boy Scouts of America, Chunky Candy Factory, Churchill Center, Coca-Cola, Continental Insurance, Demonstration Center, Du Pont, Dynamic Maturity, Equitable Life, Festival of Gas, Fiesta, First National City Bank, Formica, Johnson Wax, Julimar Farm, Mastro Pizza, Mormon Church, National Cash Register, Oregon, Pavilion of American Interiors, Pool of Industry, Protestant and Orthodox Center, Radio Corporation of America, Russian Orthodox Greek-Catholic Church, Schaefer, Scott Paper, 7-Up, Simmons, Singer Bowl, Tiparillo Band & US Post Office.

Assorted milk caps. $4-5 ea.

Assorted pins. $20-30 ea.

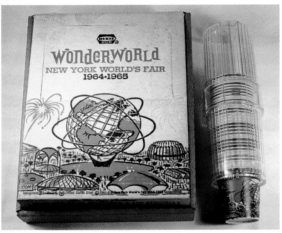

Dixie cup set with cups. $375-400.

Bumper stickers. $25-30 ea.

Large GE Progressland poster.
28" x 48". $125-175.

GE Progressland items. $10-12 ea.

GE Progressland ashtray. 4" diameter. $10-12.

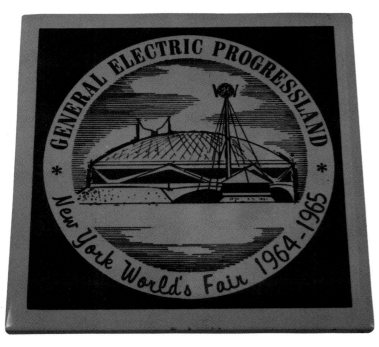

GE Progressland 45rpm record. $40-45.

GE Progressland sheet music. $20-40.

GE Progressland tile. 4.25" x 4.25". $65-75+.

Kodak Poster. 24" x 11". $75-85.

Kodak brochure with film & flash chart. $15-20.

Adams hat box. 13" x 14" x 7". $55-65.

General Cigar ashtray. 8" wide. $15-20.

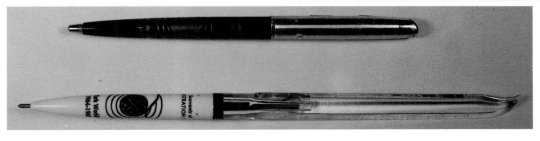

Demonstration center pens. $10-12 ea.

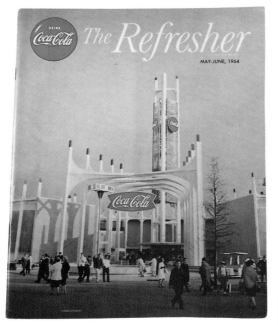

General Cigar brochures. $10-12 ea.

Coke brochures. 18-20 ea.

Coke coupon. $8-10.

Coke vinyl cooler. 10" x 9" x 6". $250-275+.

Coke bottle cap display/ad. 18" x 24". $250-300+.

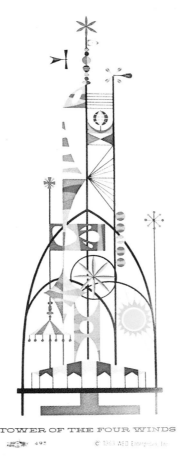

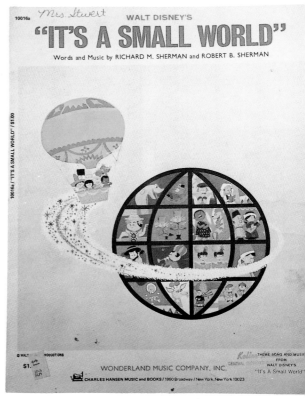

Pepsi "It's A Small World" ticket.
2" x 4.5". $8-10.

Back view of ticket.

Pepsi "It's A Small World" sheet music. $18-25.

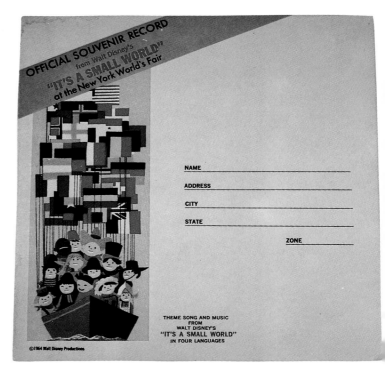

Pepsi "It's A Small World" record album. $35-40.

Pepsi "It's A Small World" 45rpm record. $30-35.

Pepsi vinyl cooler. 12" tall, 10" wide. $225-250+.

Festival of Gas soda cap. 1.5" diameter. $20-25.

Festival of Gas cufflinks. $28-30.

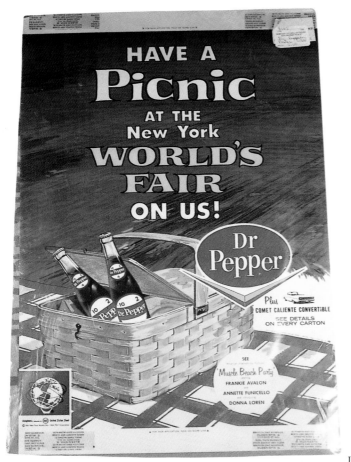

Festival of Gas set of 6 glasses & box. $150-175.

Dr. Pepper poster. 12.5" x 11.5". $95-100.

Tower of Light mirror. 3" x 2". $30-45.

Tower of Light brochures.
$10-12 ea.

Tower of Light 45 rpm records. $20-25 ea.

Tower of Light eyeglass wipes. $8-10 ea.

Tower of Light brochures, $10-12 ea.
Christmas card (*bottom left*), $20-25.

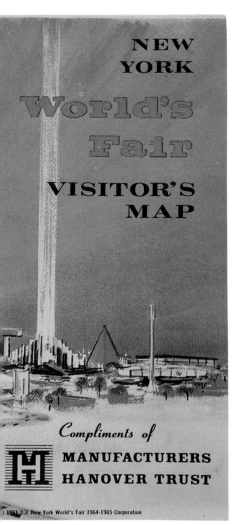

Map, front cover. 12.5" x 7". $8-10.

Mormon Bible. 5" x 7".
$18-25.

Visitor's map. $8-10.

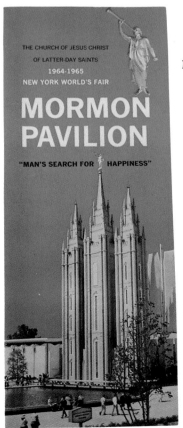

Mormon Pavilion brochure. $8-10.

Mormon Pavilion postcard. $5-6.

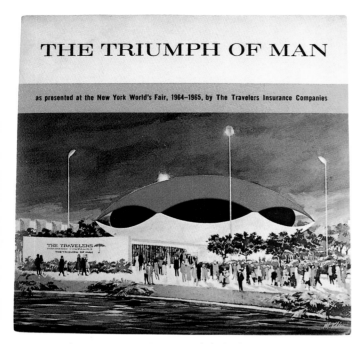

Travelers Insurance 45rpm record. $10-12.

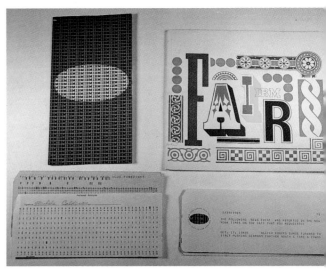

American Express 45 rpm record. $18-20.

Foster Grant display. $55-65.

American Express bag. $15-18.

American Express coins in box. $25-30.

American Express knife. $18-20.

Assorted paper napkins. $2-5 ea.

Brass Rail paper coffee cup. $15-20.

Drinks brochure. 7" x 5.5". $10-12.

Millstone Restaurant ashtray. $8-10.

Dinkelacker mug & shot. $35-45 ea.

Assorted matchcovers. $5-12 ea.

Coasters. 3.5" diameter. $2-4 ea.

Jazzland matchbook. $5-6.

Tower of Light matches. $3-5.

Bell System brochures, $12-15. Old Timers Day plaque (*lower right*), $50-75.

American Express brochures. $8-10 ea.

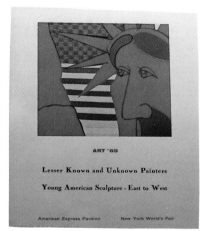

AAA brochures. $8-10 ea.

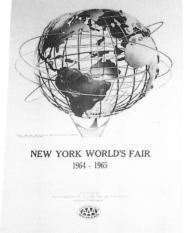

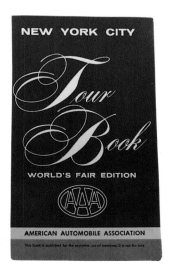

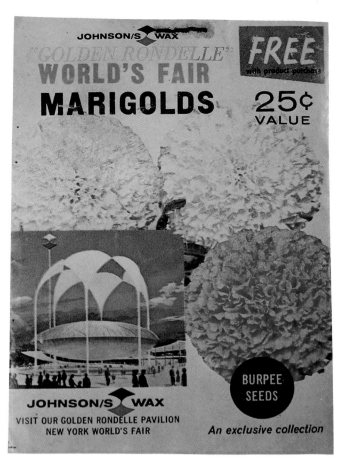

Johnson Wax marigolds seed package. $18-25+.

Du Pont 45 rpm record. $18-20.

Du Pont brochure. $5-8.

Pavilion of American Interiors brochures. $2-5 ea.

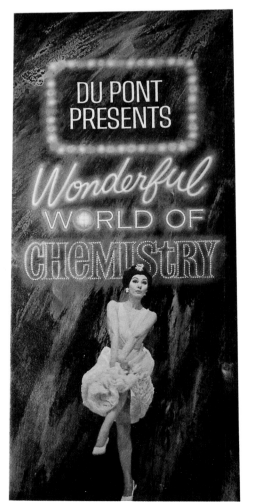

General Foods puzzle with original mailer. $30-35.

Better Living Center. Waverly fabric with original tag. $75-85.

Hotpoint cookbook. $15-18.

Better Living Center ribbon. $18-20.

Better Living Center. Hershey's tin lid. 8" diameter. $35-45.

The World's Fair House - Formica Pavilion brochure. $15-18.

Dinkelacker ashtray. 5.75" diameter. $10-12.

Better Living Center paper coasters. $8-10 ea.

Better Living Center brochures. $8-10 ea.

House of Good Taste Karosel Kitchen. Sears toy with box. $200-250+.

Elsie comic, 14 pg. 7" x 5". $25-30. Elsie ID card, $20-25.

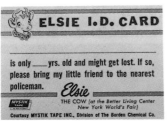

Toy Switchboard with box. Similar to one displayed at House of Good Taste. $225-250+.

Sports Illustrated ashtray. 8.25" wide. $15-20.

Foreign pavilions gave a glimpse of life on the other side of the world & showed new and exciting sites at every turn. Exotic foods, art & handicrafts never seen - except in large cities - were readily available to Fair visitors. Highlights of the International Area included:

Vatican

Visitors may view the Fair's most important work of art, Michelangelo's *Pieta*–displayed for the first time outside St. Peter's Church in Rome.

Swiss Sky Ride

Cable cars carry visitors across the Fair - high up in the sky.

Belgian Village

Shops and restaurants line the cobblestone streets in this recreation of an eighteenth-century walled village. Home of the famous "Bel-Gem" Waffle.

African Pavilion

Village of huts with exhibits ranging from tribal art to caged lions.

Other International Area Pavilions Included:

American Israel, Austria, Berlin, Billy Graham, Caribbean, Central America, Republic of China, Christian Science, Denmark, Greece, Guinea, Hall of Free Enterprise, Hong Kong, India, Indonesia, Ireland, Japan, Jordan, Republic of Korea, Malaysia, Masonic Center, Mexico, Morocco, Pakistan, Paris, Philippines, Polynesia, Sermons From Science, Spain, Sudan, Sweden, Switzerland, Thailand, Two Thousand Tribes, United Arab Republic & Venezuela.

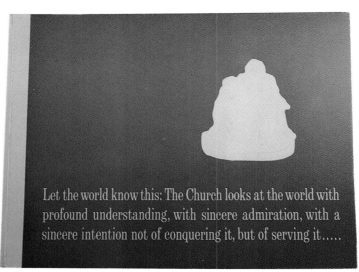

Let the world know this: The Church looks at the world with profound understanding, with sincere admiration, with a sincere intention not of conquering it, but of serving it.....

Vatican VIP presentation book. 14" x 11". $150-195.

Laminated license plate. $40-50.

Vatican Pavilion brochures. $4-5 ea.

Vatican doll. 5.5" tall in box. $55-60.

Pieta. 6" model. Resin material on wood base. $35-40.

Vatican storycards. 6" x 4". $25-30.

Vatican ceramic tile. 6" x 6". $35-40+.

Vatican tray puzzle. 10" x 14". $10-12.

Swiss Pavilion hankie. $35-40.

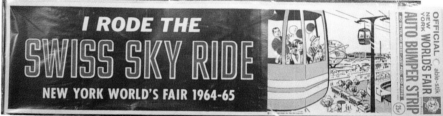

Swiss Sky Ride bumper sticker. $25-35.

Vatican coloring book. 8.5" x 11". $20-28.

Mini Bible. 2" x 2.5". $5-6.

Switzerland cutting board. 10" tall. $15-20.

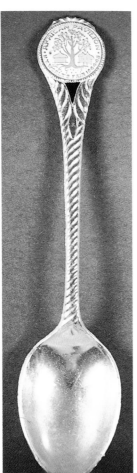

African Pavilion 11" plastic spoon. $15-18.

Polynesian Pavilion sugar packet. $12-15.

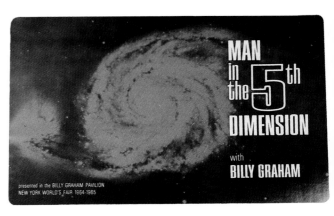

Billy Graham Pavilion brochures. $4-5 ea.

Cufflinks. African Pavilion, Billy Graham & Money Tree. $18-20 pair.

Billy Graham cufflinks. $15-18 pr.

Billy Graham keychain with Bible quotes. $20-25.

America-Israel bookmark. 11" long. $10-12.

American-Israel tie clip. $25-30.

Apocalypse book. $8-10.

Austria brochures, $5-8 ea. Cloth patch, $10-12.

Belgian Village mini 2" lantern. $55-65.

BELGIAN TERRACE CAFE

Belgian Village tickets, $2-5 ea. Menu, $30-40.

Denmark Pavilion toothpick holder. 2" x 2". $15-18.

German Pavilion ashtray. 5" x 5". $8-10.

Sweden Pavilion paperweight. 2" x 2". $15-18.

Korean Pavilion silk purse. $20-25.

Swedish Pavilion pin. $5-10.

Korean Pavilion 4" letter opener. $18-25.

Hand fans. Large, $55-65. Small, $25-35.

Hong Kong dragon pin. 2" wide. $35-40.

Japan Pavilion chopsticks. $12-15.

Hitachi flicker pin. 3" diameter. $15-20.

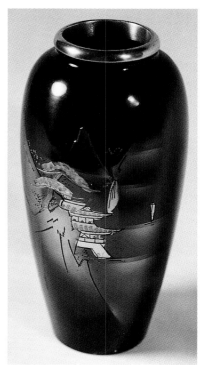

Hong Kong Pavilion metal vase. 6" tall. $35-40.

Hong Kong Pavilion book, $20-25. Drink menu, $15-20.

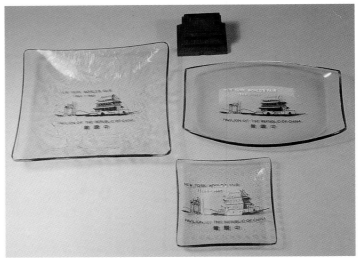

China Pavilion ashtrays. $8-10 ea.

Guinea Pavilion matchbook. $5-6.

Hong Kong Pavilion 4" wood figure. $55-65.

Armenian Festival programs. $12-15 ea.

Hall of Education ceramic tile. 4" x 4". $30-35.

Venzuela Pavilion 2" wood vase. $25-30.

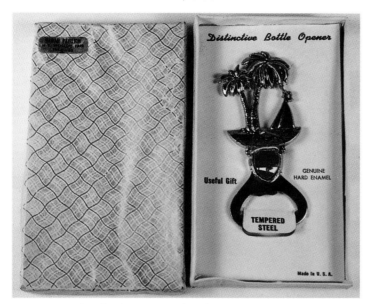

Hawaii Pavilion bottle opener in box. $25-30.

Hall of Free Enterprise cork coasters in wood holder. $18-25 set.

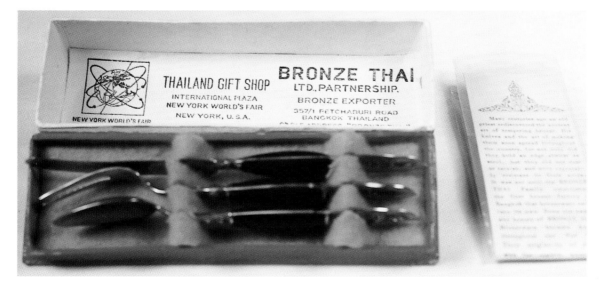

Thailand 4" utensil set in box. $25-30.

Hall of Free Enterprise ashtray. $10-12.

Mexican Pavilion leather cigarette case. $10-12.

Spain Pavilion brochures. $2-4 ea.

India Pavilion tea tins. 3.5" x 2.5". $45-55 ea.

Indonesia Pavilion Menu. $35-40+.

Japan ceramic tile. 6" x 6". $35-45.

Unisphere

Author Joyce Grant at the 1964 NY World's Fair.

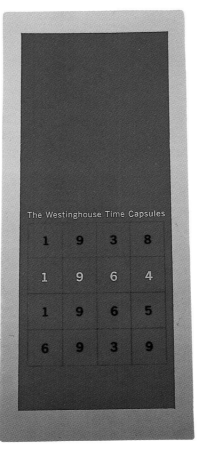

The Westinghouse Time Capsules

1 9 3 8
1 9 6 4
1 9 6 5
6 9 3 9

Westinghouse Time Capsules brochure (*left*), $2-4. Pin (*right*), $5-8.

The *Unisphere* was the centerpiece of the Fair and was located in the Federal & State Area. Every World's Fair photo album has at least one shot of a family member in front of it. Created by Gilmore Clarke, the *Unisphere* was chosen as the Fair's logo for its simplicity and universal appeal. US Steel constructed it in exchange for the publicity. The *Unisphere* is the largest model of the Earth ever made. It is 140 ft. tall and was constructed from 250 tons of steel gracefully balanced on an open, three-prong pedestal. The continents are represented on the surface of the steel sphere, which is encircled by three giant rings denoting the first manmade satellites that launched the space age. The *Unisphere* is one of the few Fair structures still remaining at Flushing Meadows Park.

New York State

Glass tube elevators climb up the Fair's tallest observation towers. Below, various displays are sheltered under the world's largest suspension roof, made of translucent colored plastic and hung from sixteen 100-foot concrete columns. On the main floor is a huge in-laid terrazzo map of NY state.

New York City

Huge scale model of New York City on display. Cost $600,000 and took 2 years to build. 835,000 buildings are shown. The panoramic display still remains at Flushing Meadows Park in the building that is now The Queens Museum Of Art.

Hollywood, USA

Behind Grauman's Chinese Theatre facade, see actual movie displays and celebrities.

Illinois

Walt Disney designed the Audio-Animatronic of Abe Lincoln for this pavilion.

Westinghouse

Time Capsule buried 50 ft. underground, to be opened 5,000 years later. Contents of the capsule included: *Plastic Heart Valve, Transistor Radio, Contact Lenses, Ballpoint Pen, Rechargeable Flashlight, Polaroid Camera, Freeze Dried Food, Birth Control Pills, Computer Memory Unit, Electric Toothbrush, Electronic Watch, Beatles Record, Bikini, Filtered Cigarettes, Tranquilizers, Antibiotics, Credit Card, Irradiated Seeds, Fifty-star American Flag, and Bible.*

Other Federal & State Pavilions Included:

Alaska, Long Island Railroad, Maryland, Minnesota, Missouri, Montana, New England States, New Jersey, New Mexico, Oklahoma, United States, West Virginia & Wisconsin.

NY State Pavilion keychain. $15-18.

NY State Pavilion bowl in original box. 4.5" diameter. $28-30.

Federal Pavilion brochures. $5-8 ea.

NY State Pavilion bumpersticker. 4.5" x 8.5". $15-18.

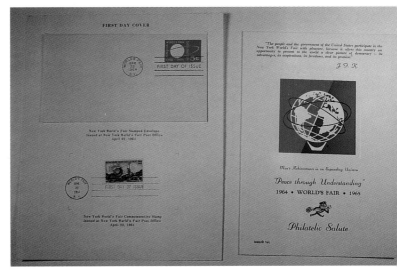

US Postal First Day Cover. $12-20.

US Postage stamps & ad. $30-35.

West Virginia brochures. $5-8 ea.

Wisconsin brochures, $5-8. Menu, $15-18.

West Virginia Day plaque. $30-40.

New England Pavilion jar lid. $15-18.

Alaska Pavilion plastic 2.5" figures. $18-20 ea.

Illinois Pavilion Lincoln bust.
3" tall. $20-25.

Montana Pavilion
brochures. $5-8 ea.

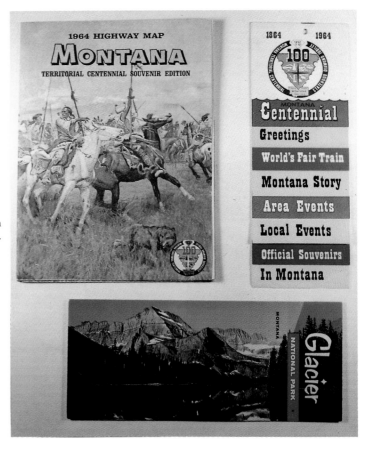

Walt Disney's autograph on Illinois
Pavilion brochure. $95-125+.

Texas Pavilion 3.5" mug. $10-12.

Louisiana Pavilion crackle glass 3.5" pitcher. $28-35.

Maryland Pavilion aluminum
cup. 4.75" tall. $12-15.

Hollywood Pavilion, Stan
Johnson print on masonite.
12" x 20". $55-65+.

Masonic badge. 5" long. $65-75.

Ashtray with masonic emblem. 5" x 4". $15-18.

Masonic ashtray. 5.25" x 5.25". $15-18.

Oklahoma glass dish. 5.75" x 2.75". $12-15.

New Mexico steakhouse discount ticket. 6" x 2". $5-6.

Major auto makers as well as other transportation companies were represented here. New car models could be seen and "driven" by Fair visitors. Highlights of the Transportation Area included:

Sinclair Dinoland

Nine life-sized dinosaurs displayed in realistic prehistoric settings. The largest were animated. Visitors could mold their own mini dinosaur for 10 cents.

US Rubber

Plastic gondolas transport guests around an 80 ft. high tire.

Ford

Visitors ride in Ford cars along a track to view animated displays of man's progress from the prehistoric times to the space age. Lucky visitors get to ride in a new 1964 Mustang!

General Motors-Futurama

Sitting in contoured seats equipped with speakers, visitors move past animated scenes of life on the moon, under the sea, in the jungle, and on the desert. Exhibit shows future technology.

US Space Park

Sponsored by NASA and Dept. of Defense. Space ships and rockets are displayed.

Chrysler

Huge engine model that visitors can walk through.

Avis Antique Car Ride

Visitors can ride in antique models of cars on scenic roadways.

Auto Thrill Show

Stunt drivers perform auto stunts at high speeds.

Greyhound

Travel exhibits. Ride the Glide-A-Ride instead of walking.

Other Transportation Area Attractions Included:

Eastern Air Lines, Hall of Science, Hertz, Lowenbrau Gardens, NMU Park, Port Authority Heliport, SKF, Socony Mobil, Transportation and Travel, and Underground Home.

American Airlines poster. 29" x 39". $250-275+.

Eastern Airlines passenger magazine. 9" x 9". $25-30.

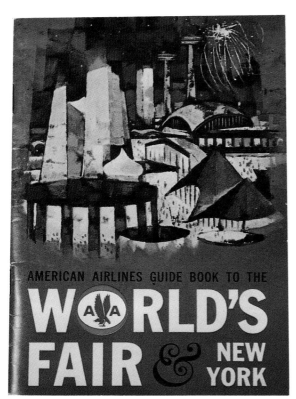

AMERICAN AIRLINES GUIDE BOOK TO THE
WORLD'S FAIR & NEW YORK

United Air Lines brochures. $18-22 ea.

American Airlines Guide Book to the Fair, 66 pages. 4" x 6". $10-12.

GATEWAY TO THE WORLD'S FAIR

Unisphere® presented by USS United States Steel © 1961 New York World's Fair 1964-1965 Corporation

Pan Am wallet calendar. $5-8.

WORLD'S FAIR SUBWAY MAP

FOLLOW THE BLUE ARROW—Connecting lines from up-town or downtown Manhattan, the Bronx, Brooklyn and other parts of Queens have free transfer points to the World's Fair Line. Follow the Blue Arrow, prominently displayed throughout the subway system.

NY Subway map. $18-22.

Long Island Railroad.
Ticket & pin. $35-40.

Pennsylvania Railroad flyers. $18-20 ea.

NY Port Authority - "Top of The Fair" menu. $35-40.

Sikorsky helicopter 3" pin. $45-50.

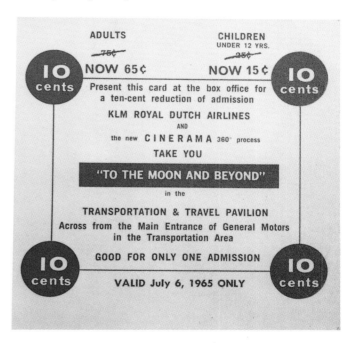

Transportation & Travel Pavilion ticket. $5-10.

Transportation & Travel Pavilion program. $50-60.

Chrysler Dodge items.
$10-12 ea.

Sinclair sign. 2.5" x 2".
$10-12.

Dodge banner. 7' long. $175-200+.

US Royal Tire brochure &
ticket. $10-12 ea.

US Royal Tire battery
operated mechanical
toy with box. 12" tall.
$375-425+.

Dinoland booklet. $20-25.

Sinclair sticker. 2" x 3". $4-5.

Sinclair dinosaurs. Approx. 5" tall. $45-50+ ea.

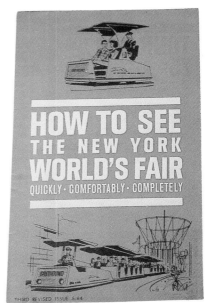

Greyhound ticket lot. $5-6.

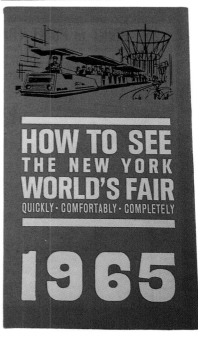

Greyhound maps. $5-10 ea.

Greyhound luggage tag. Paper, 4" x 1.5". $8-10.

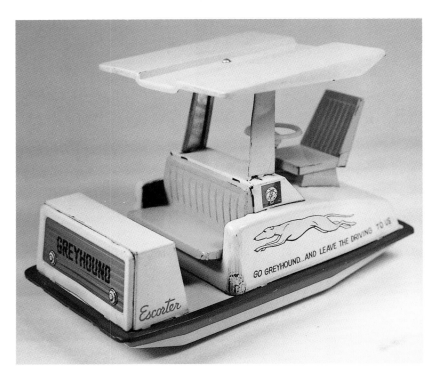

Greyhound tin friction toy. *Escorter*. 6" long. $450-500+.

Greyhound "Glide-A-Ride" friction toy with box. 9" long. $375-450+.

Greyhound Bus Travel boardgame. $95-125.

Trailways brochure, $15-18. Ticket envelope, $12-15.

General Motors brochures. $15-18 ea.

General Motors playing cards. $20-25.

General Motors
paperweight. 3".
$18-20.

GM Futurama brochure. $12-15.

Chrysler VIP cardboard
pin. 4" long. $5-8.

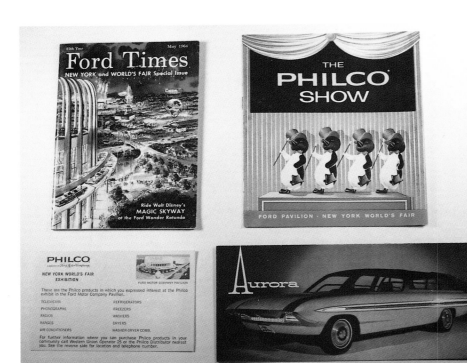

Assorted maps. $10-12.

Ford Pavilion brochures. $12-15 ea.

Ford glow-in-the-dark plastic badges. 2.5" x 1.5". $6-8 ea.

Assorted maps. $10-15.

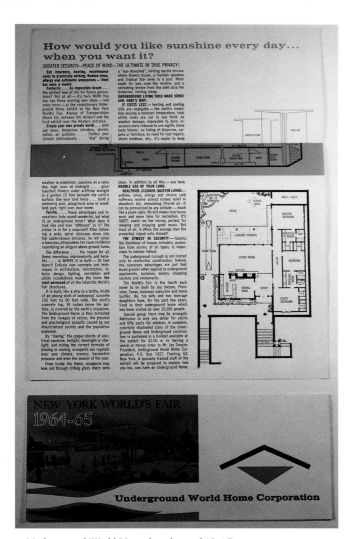

Underground World Home brochure. $12-15.

Hall of Science brochures. $8-10 ea.

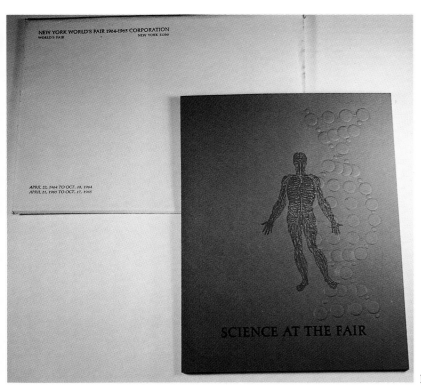

Irradiated dime. $15-18.

Hall of Science booklet. $10-12.

Located on the other side of the Long Island Expressway & next to Meadow Lake, visitors could experience water shows and other attractions in a carnival atmosphere.

AMF Monorail

Two car trains, hung from an overhead rail, circle the Lake area 40 feet off the ground.

Amphicar Ride

Amphibious autos carry passengers down a ramp to the lake and back to land.

Log Flume Ride

Four passengers in dugout boats swoosh along a watery roller coaster and splash into a pool.

Jaycopter Ride

A 16-passenger cabin on a 100-foot boom simulates a helicopter flight.

Santa Maria

Authentic replica of Columbus' flagship.

Florida/Florida Citrus Water Show

Tourist attractions, porpoises, and water shows.

Hawaii

Exotic dances and music with handicrafts for tourists.

Walters Wax Museum

160 life-like figures on display, the largest collection in the US.

Other Areas of Interest Included:

Aerial Tower Ride, Carnival, Carousel Park, Dancing Waters, Funland, Lake Cruise, Les Poupees De Paris & Thrill Rides.

Family Fun brochure, front. $2-4.

Johnson Marina print. 9" x 11". $18-22.

The thrilling Log Flume ride

"Meadow Lake" sheet music. $35-40.

Here's how a family of 4 spent
an exciting day for only $7.46 —
including lunch and dinner!
(excluding Fair admission)

The New York World's Fair offers a world of fun for the whole family to enjoy together, and it can be surprisingly inexpensive. Look how much this did—for so little. • Watched themselves on Color television at the RCA pavilion. **Free** • Saw fabulous jeweled carpet at the pavilion of India. **Free** • Visited replica of Thailand's *Temple of Dawn.* **Free** • Rode through General Motors' "Futurama II." **Free** • Viewed Michelangelo's "Pieta" at Vatican pavilion. **Free** • Took a ride along Ford's "Magic Skyway." **Free** • Ate four generous slices of Carousel Park pizza. **25¢** each • Had four Cokes. **10¢** each • Drove in Avis antique cars. **35¢**, children; **50¢** adults • Rode the "People Wall" at IBM's pavilion. **Free** • Viewed New York City on simulated helicopter ride in New York City pavilion. **10¢** each • Watched the magic show at General Cigar. **Free** • Marveled at the "flying bird-men" at the Mexican exhibit—and the native dances that followed. **Free** • Heard pop concert at Singer Bowl; then saw million-dollar fabric collection. **Free** • Had four full-course Chinese dinners at Chun King restaurant. **99¢** each • Saw dancers and singers at the New York State pavilion. **Free** • Heard the incredibly lifelike Lincoln talk at the Illinois pavilion. **Free** • Enjoyed the porpoise show at the Florida pavilion. **Free** • Looked at

Family Fun brochure, inside. $2-4.

Monorail stand-up poster. 13" x 17". $65-75+.

Monorail Pioneer cloth patch. 2" x 2". $12-15.

Monorail brochures & tickets. $10-18 ea.

"See The Fair" sheet music. $25-30.

Santa Maria change purse.
2.5" x 2". $18-22.

Discotheque discount
card. $5-10.

Santa Maria scarf. $40-45.

Santa Maria tile. 4.5" x 4.5". $20-22.

Santa Maria plastic wall plaque. $40-45.

Florida trophy. 5" tall. $18-20.

Santa Maria dish. 4.5" diameter. $18-20.

Helldrivers ticket. $8-10.

Florida Pavilion paperweights. $20-25 ea.

Florida Pavilion pin. 3" diameter. $12-15.

Florida brochures. $5-8.

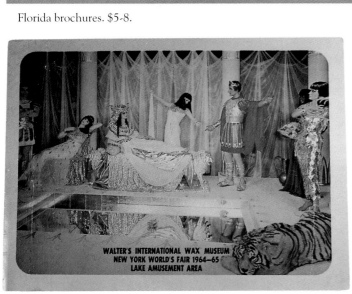

Mini Lai. 2" x 3" in box. $18-20.

Wax Museum program, $25-30.
Coupon, $5-8.

Hawaii Pavilion brochures. $2-4.

Continental Circus program. 8.5" x 11". $30-35.

Hawaii Pavilion coaster sets. $10-12 ea.

1964 Amphicar. $35,000+.

Items used in the everyday operations of the Fair are highly sought after by collectors. Admission tickets, ticket bags, signs, uniforms, posters, even bricks from demolished buildings are very desirable.

Operations Manual. $75-85+.

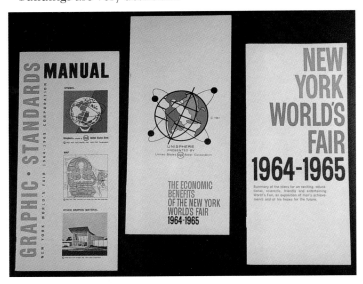

Planning brochures. $75-85 ea.

1959 letterheads. $12-15 ea.

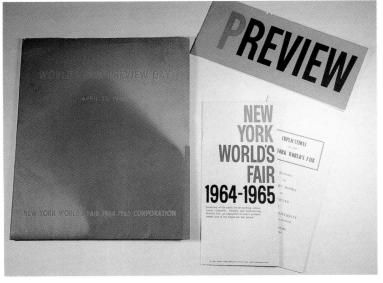

1961 Press Preview Pack. $175-200+.

Press Info Kit. $100-125+.

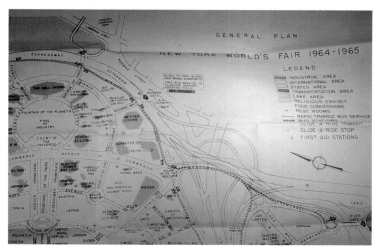

General Plan blueprint. $100-125+.

US Steel brochures. $10-12 ea.

Unisphere model. 21" x 16". $2,000-2,500+.

Unisphere construction plans. $100-150+.

Fair News bulletin. $12-15.

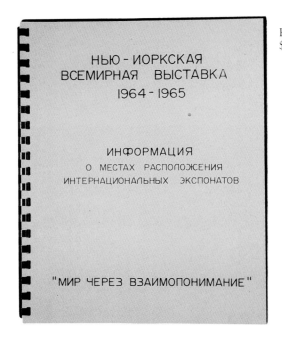

Russian promo booklet. $75-85.

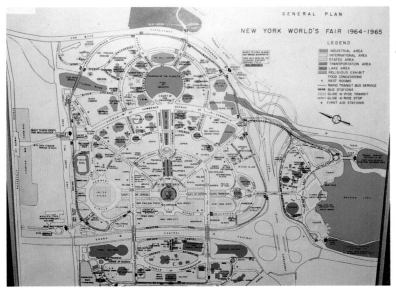

ID card for construction vehicles. 5" x 7". $18-20.

NY Telephone porcelain booth sign. 20" x 20". $250-300+.

Laminated general map with legend. 4.5' x 3.5'. 2,000-2,250+.

Metal subway sign. 22.5" wide. $250-300+.

Subway sign converted into a spoon rack. 36" tall. $100-125+.

Metal highway sign. 29" long. $200-250+.

Admission tickets. $15-20 ea.

Postcard sign. 18" x 17". $55-75.

Top left, top center and bottom left photo: Brochure display. 11" x 16". $55-65.

Official ceremony tickets. $20-25 ea.

"Official Party" pin. $18-20.

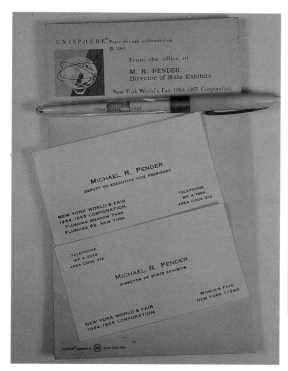

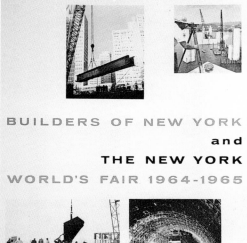

Builders of the Fair book. 8.5" x 11". $25-45.

Desk items. $10-30+ ea.

Promotional photos. 8" x 10". $25-30 ea.

Assorted wallet cards. $5-8 ea.

Color chart. 6" x 11". $18-20.

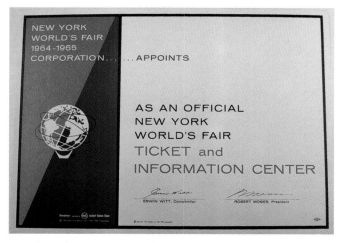

Ticket info sign. 11" x 14". $150-175.

Promo sign. 25" x 9.5". $125-150.

Hotel brochure. $5-8.

Transit card. 11" x 28". $125-150.

Discount coupon book. $10-12.

Welcome banner. 16" x 18" $48-55.

Discount books. $10-12 ea.

City Service World's Fair Band & Nixon photo with Nixon's autograph. $150+.

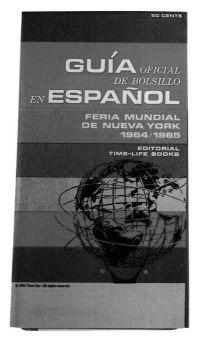

Various promo guides. $25-40 ea.

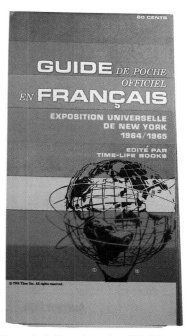

Spanish & French guides. $20-25 ea.

Lamp banner. 7' long. $250-300+.

NY edition WF guides. $12-15 ea.

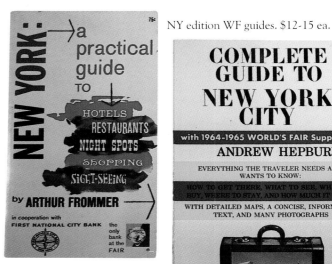

Spain Pavilion guides. $25-40 ea.

Re-Opening Day program with Moses' autograph. $100-150+.

Flying and *Flower Grower*
magazine. $25-30 ea.

Pinkerton magazine. $25-30.

New Yorker magazine. $25-30.

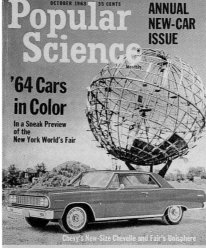

Popular Science magazine. $25-30.

Time magazine with Moses
on cover. $35-40.

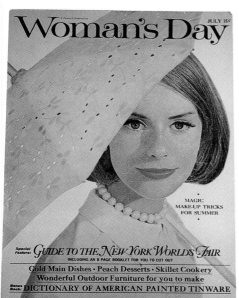

Woman's Day magazine. $25-30.

Post magazine. $20-22.

Promotional film with case. 13" x 13". $100-150+.

National Geographic. $25-30.

1965 Young Peoples book. $18-22.

Girls magazine. $20-22.

═══153═══

License plate. $30-40.

Various tickets. $5-8 ea.

1964 advertising calendar. $20-25.

1964 Macy's Christmas gift boxes. $25-40 ea.

Olympic trials program. $35-50.

1964 All-star game program. $175-200+.

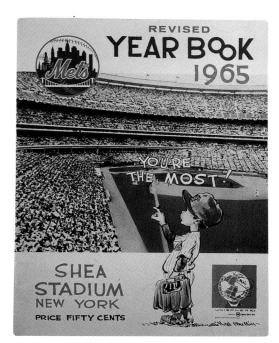

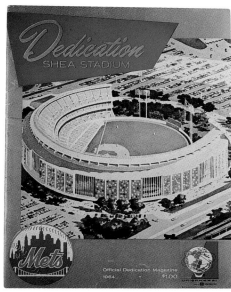

1964 *Dedication Shea Stadium* magazine. $125-150+.

"Ice Travaganza" sheet music. $25-30 ea.

1965 Mets Yearbook. $50-75.

1964 Mets Yearbook. $50-75.

1964 Mets program. $20-25.

Boy Scout neckerchief. $65-75.

Boy Scout patches. $40-50 ea.

Mason pin. $35-45.

Boy Scout leather neckerchief slide. $20-25.

Terrace Club car plaque. $125-175.

Boy Scout neckerchief slides. $25-30 ea.

Paperweight. 4" x 3". $20-25.

Employee costume top. $250-300.

VIP Limo - back window plaque. Metal, 6" x 4.5". $150-200.

WORLD'S FAIR CORPORATION
TRIBOROUGH BRIDGE AND TUNNEL AUTHORITY
DEPARTMENT OF PARKS
FLUSHING MEADOWS-CORONA PARK
JUNE 3rd, 1967

Park & WF employee presentation piece. 4" x 5". $75-85.

Greyhound employee patch. 2.5" x 4". $25-30.

Employee patches. $18-25 ea.

General Motors employee pin. $75-85.

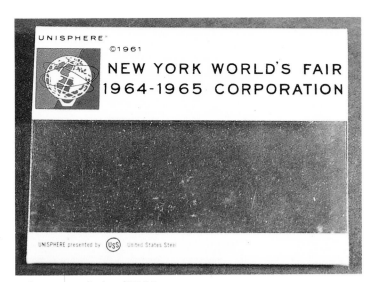

Corporation badge. $25-30.

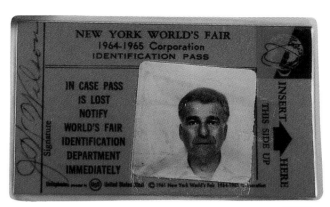

General Motors employee badge & pass. $60-65 pr.

Assorted NY Police badges. $1,500-$2,000 ea.

Employee ID card. $25-30+.

Maintenance badge. 2" wide. $60-75.

Greyhound employee ladies' jacket. $250-275+.

Greyhound employee men's jacket. $250-275+.

Brick from demolished Amphitheater (with certificate of authenticity). $15-20.

Hard hat from dismantling of Spanish Pavilion, front. $55-65.

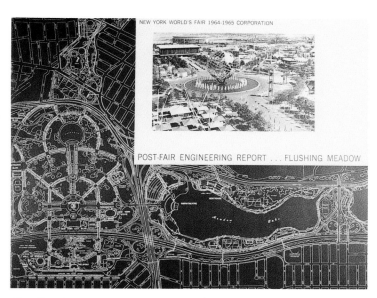

Post-Fair Engineering Report. 8.5" x 11". $55-60.

Hard hat, back view.

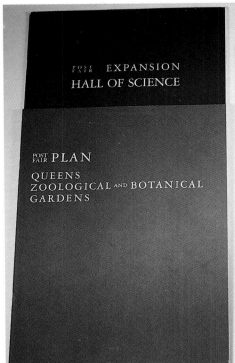
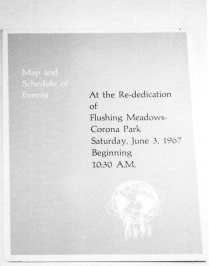

Post Fair material. $65-75 ea.

Fair close-out catalog. $75-100+.

Bibliography

1964 OFFICIAL GUIDE TO NY WORLD'S FAIR. New York: Time Inc., 1961.

REMEMBERING THE FUTURE: NY WORLD'S FAIR FROM 1939-1964. Introduction by Robert Rosenblum: essays by Rosemarie Haag Bletter. New York: Rizzoli International Publications, 1989.

Sources for 1964-65 NY World's Fair Items

The following is a list of locations where World's Fair items may be purchased.

Queens Museum - Gift Shop
NYC Building, Flushing Meadow Park
Flushing, NY 11368

TimeWarp Toys & Collectibles
PO Box 632
Phoenicia, NY 12464
http://www.timewarp-toys.com

World's Fair Collector's Society
PO Box 20806
Sarasota, FL 34276-3806
email: WFCS@aol.com

Yesterdays World
Herb Rolfes
PO Box 398
Mount Dora, FL 32756
(352) 735-3947